❁ The ❁
SCHOOLMASTERS

This New England Primer *was published in 1737. This is its actual size.*
(Beinecke Rare Book Manuscript Library, Yale University.)

COLONIAL AMERICANS

The

SCHOOLMASTERS

WRITTEN & ILLUSTRATED BY

Leonard Everett Fisher

FRANKLIN WATTS

New York / London

To the American schoolteacher

SBN 531-01034-1

Library of Congress Catalog Card Number: 67-18896
© Copyright 1967 by Leonard Everett Fisher
Printed in the United States of America

❀ The ❀
SCHOOLMASTERS

The New England Primer, *first published in 1690, was used as a textbook in New England schools for about one hundred years. This one, photographed in its actual size, was printed in the 1700's. (The Pequot Library Collection, Southport, Connecticut.)*

n July 4, 1776, the thirteen British colonies in America tore themselves loose from their mother country and proclaimed their freedom, saying:

"We, therefore, the Representatives of the United States of America, in General Congress, Assembled, appealing to the Supreme Judge of the world for the rectitude of our intentions do, in the Name, and by Authority of the good People of these Colonies, solemnly publish and declare, That these United Colonies are, and of Right ought to be Free and Independent States . . ."

On that summer day almost two hundred years ago the world changed, although many people did not realize it at the time. The change had been coming for 169 years in the American colonies and for centuries in other places, but it finally happened almost as suddenly as if someone had turned off a light in one room and turned on a light in another.

"We hold these truths to be self-evident," declared the colonists in America, "that all men are created equal, that they are endowed by their Creator with certain unalienable Rights, that

*Upper-class people in the Middle Ages
expected lower-class people
to bow down before them.*

among these are Life, Liberty, and the pursuit of Happiness."

That, right there, was the change. It was the idea that all people are equal and have the right to liberty. This idea was a frightful shock to rulers in the Old World. It meant that the people had the right to decide how and by whom they would be governed. To many members of the government in England this was an impossible idea — one that they felt must be stopped at all costs.

During the Middle Ages, the people of the Old World had been divided into two main groups, or classes. A small number — royalty, nobles, aristocracy, and church officials — belonged to the upper, or governing, class. The greater number, including beggars, thieves, apprentices, craftsmen, farmers, servants, and the like, belonged to the lower, or governed, class.

The people who were governed had very little to say about anything — least of all about the upper class who ruled them. The upper class had a great deal to say about everything — most of all about the people they ruled. The upper class owned almost all the land that the lower class walked on, worked on, and lived on.

During the fifteenth and sixteenth centuries the world suddenly seemed to grow larger. Explorers were finding new lands and were bringing silver, gold, furs, and other riches back to Europe. Merchant adventurers, making the most of this new situation, began to grow wealthy themselves. They and the tradesmen they dealt with were not members of the upper class. Gradually they formed another class, which had a position between the upper and the lower classes. It was the middle class. Its members saw the possibilities of their new wealth, and soon they began to make their power felt. But, for the most part, the upper class still had the upper hand. A great many people still believed that the members of the upper class and of the Church were meant to lead and that the rest of the population was meant to follow.

The members of the upper class did nothing to discourage this idea. They felt that if too many of the other people became well educated they would be difficult to govern. So, usually, the young people of the upper class, and a few other promising scholars, received the really good education that would fit them for positions of authority. The less fortunate people received less education — often just enough so that they could go on working at their jobs and in their shops, remaining obedient to the laws of the government and the particular church that the government approved.

Because of this arrangement there were no free public schools as we know them today. There were few books and even fewer good teachers. Those parents who wanted their children to know how to read and write had to see to it themselves that the young were taught. Some parents, if they themselves could read and write, did their own teaching. Some parents, if they had enough money, hired a traveling, or itinerant, teacher or a neighbor who could take on the task. Some parents sent their children to church schools where they learned to read and to recite their prayers, but were taught little else.

Most of the schools of Europe and England were attended by boys only. At school the boys were usually treated as horrible little creatures who needed whippings more than learning, in order to keep them from the Devil's ways. Girls, for the most part, escaped school, since they were kept at home to learn weaving, sewing, cooking, and other homemaking skills, as well as the alphabet.

During the seventeenth century two English religious groups, the Separatists and the Puritans, established colonies on the lonely shores of Massachusetts. The settlers brought with them many of their Old World ideas. They believed that the people should obey the government and the Church. But, although they were loyal to the British Crown, they disapproved of the official Church of England. The Separatists, who settled Plymouth, wished to separate entirely from the Church of England. The Puritans, who settled Boston, wished only to "purify" that church by making reforms. Rather than stay in their homeland where they would be persecuted for not following the established ways of religion, many of the Separatists and Puritans came to America. There, in a new country, they founded their own churches according to their own ideas. There, too, they hoped to find better opportunities for advancing themselves.

*Prayer and religion were
of first importance to the
early New Englanders.*

During the first years of colonization the Separatists and the Puritans were so busy working to stay alive, and praying to the Almighty to keep them from harm, that they paid little attention to education. Even so, they spent some thought on it — most especially on the problem of finding new church ministers to take the places of those who died.

"After God had carried us safe to New England and we had builded our houses, provided necessaries for our livelihood, reared convenient places for God's worship and settled the civil government, one of the next things we longed for and looked after was to advance learning and perpetuate it to posterity, dreading to leave an illiterate ministry to the churches when our present ministers shall lie in the dust," wrote one man at that time.

In 1635, fifteen years after the Pilgrims arrived at Plymouth, five years after the founding of Boston, and two years after the Dutch opened a free reading school for everyone in Fort Amsterdam, the Puritans founded America's first formal school for boys, known as the Boston Latin Gram-

mar School. Because the tuition was high, only the sons of moneyed families were sent to this school, where they began studying for the ministry. From the ages of eight to sixteen the boys learned Greek, Latin, reading, and writing. Out of this school and a number of other Latin grammar schools founded in New England over the next sixty-five years the best students went on to Harvard College or to the Collegiate School, which later became Yale College. The young men who completed their studies at these colleges became ministers of the Puritan, or Congregational, Church, as well as leaders in the affairs of the colonies.

The Church of England, or Anglican Church, also had a college in America, founded in 1693 at Williamsburg, Virginia. It was named the College of William and Mary, after the then reigning king and queen of England.

Having made sure that they would not be left without clergymen, the colonists next turned their attention to the matter of educating their young children.

The Puritans believed that the authorities of

their civil government and of their church should think, say, and act for the community. They also believed that the civil government's chief job was to protect the Church and enforce its regulations. Schools and schoolmasters were looked upon mostly as a means of keeping religious faith strong, rather than as a means of advancing knowledge.

In New England it was felt that everyone should be able to read the Bible and should know the laws. Accordingly, in 1642, the Massachusetts General Court passed a law requiring that "all youth be taught to read perfectly the English tongue, have knowledge in the laws and be taught some orthodox catechism." (A catechism was a series of questions and answers used in teaching religion.) The law of 1642 left it to parents and to the guardians of orphans to instruct the children. If the parents and guardians did not do this, they were fined and their children were apprenticed to a craftsman who, in addition to teaching them his craft, would also give them lessons in reading and religion.

This education law did not work out very well,

Traveling schoolmasters sometimes
taught the children.

however. Most parents were busy struggling to make a living and could not spend time in teaching. Most craftsmen were not interested in instructing young people in reading and religion. Here and there a stranger calling himself a schoolmaster would appear in a town or village. For a small fee or a night's lodging he would provide some lessons, moving on to another town almost as quickly as he had arrived at the first one. The children were a bit better off after he had gone, but not much.

The best and more learned teachers were too busy teaching the children of important families at such schools as the Boston Latin Grammar School or the free Syms School in Virginia to pay any attention to the rest of the boys and girls. Besides, these well-educated men thought it a waste of their time and knowledge to teach reading and hymn-singing to children who would never have any use for Latin and Greek.

Still, a simple education had to be provided for everyone, in order to make sure that each person could be usefully employed in the new land, that he would be obedient to the civil government and

the Church, and that he could read his Bible. It was the same Old World idea all over again: those who governed received more education; those who were governed received less.

In 1647 the Massachusetts authorities passed another law that required every town of fifty families or more to choose a teacher from among their number and provide some sort of wages for him. This law also required towns of one hundred families or more to build a Latin grammar school to prepare youths for the colleges. If the towns did not obey the law, they were fined five pounds — about twenty-five dollars. In those days it was often simpler to obey the law than to raise the money for the fine. Although many towns ignored the law entirely, still there were more schoolhouses built on the edges of the village greens than there were proper schoolmasters to man them. In New England, education became a public, or town, affair, with public schoolhouses.

In the Middle Colonies — Delaware, New York, New Jersey, and Pennsylvania — education was not public, but was left to the various church groups and the royal governor. They hired

their own schoolmasters and set up their own schools. In the South, as the tobacco plantations grew and the planters became wealthy their land-holdings spread out and there was usually no central school. The children of the richer planters were taught at home, often by tutors who came from England. Sometimes several planters joined together to form a neighborhood school for the young. The children of the poor were usually apprenticed to a craftsman, who was supposed to give them some education.

In any event, the job of teaching young children was not thought to require much knowledge. A teacher in the Latin grammar schools must have a college education, but a schoolmaster in the Colonial elementary schools needed no special study. Anyone who could read and write was allowed to teach, provided he was a strict believer in the ways of the established church, took an oath of loyalty to the Crown, and kept out of mischief. Many towns had written qualifications for their teacher. One town demanded that he be "a sober man, of good conversation." Another town asked that he be "a sober person of good

morals." Often the local minister was asked to pass judgment on the town teacher and to approve him.

Among others, indentured servants, bound to a master by contract for a number of years, became schoolmasters in order to earn enough money to buy their freedom. Quite often, clergymen in the villages took to teaching in order to earn extra money. Shopkeepers became teachers if no one else could be found. Housewives opened schools in their own kitchens. There, for a small fee, they taught very young boys and girls their ABC's and some religion. These home schools taught by women were called dame schools.

Except in the dame schools and in some of the neighborhood schools that were run by the wives of plantation owners in the South, teachers in Colonial times were almost always men — schoolmasters, not schoolmistresses. More often than not, the schoolmaster was a young man in his early twenties, though the ages of Colonial teachers might range anywhere from seventeen to seventy.

For the most part, the job was looked upon as

a lowly and easy one. Teaching in the town school was not ordinarily considered a full-time occupation. Often the schoolmaster could be seen digging graves, running errands, ringing the church bell, or leading the choir. He was not paid for these chores. They were extras, forced upon him by the town officials, and he did not like them one bit.

The average school day was sometimes eight hours long in summer, though it might be only four hours long during the dark days of winter. The school year varied, too. Some communities had only two months of school annually, while others kept classes on six days of the week for the full twelve months.

Although positions in the larger Latin grammar schools were sometimes well paid, the schoolmaster's salary was usually very small. Because the pay was so meager, many a Colonial schoolmaster became a tavern keeper in his spare hours in order to keep from starving to death. More often than not, for his services the teacher received a cow, a pig, a bushel of apples, or some other item of food instead of money.

Some schoolmasters were loaned a small piece of the public land, on which they could raise food. Other schoolmasters were hired on the promise that they could live in a rent-free house and decide how much money each family with schoolchildren was to pay them. This was a fine idea. The trouble with it was that the teacher got the house, but hardly ever collected all the money. During the cold of winter, the schoolmaster's fee was sometimes paid with a load of wood for the school fireplace. The child who failed to furnish his share of the wood was made to sit in the coldest part of the room.

Sometimes the schoolmaster "boarded around" from house to house among the families of his pupils, staying for a short while at each house. That is why some communities preferred a schoolmaster who was young and single, rather than one who was older and had a family.

None of the circumstances of a schoolmaster's life was such as to improve his temper. Often schoolmasters spent more time in trying to discipline their students than they did in teaching them to read. Some towns had great difficulty in

getting anyone at all to teach in their school-houses. The bigger boys amused themselves by thrashing the schoolmasters and kicking them out of town. Only the strongest and toughest men could handle these unruly boys. If a brawny teacher happened to be a clergyman too, so much the better. In addition to using the whipping post or the pillory — a wooden frame through which an offender had to thrust his hands and head for punishment — the clergyman was able to frighten the wits out of his pupils with threats of Hell's fire.

The schoolroom was usually an empty-looking place. There were no blackboards, chalk, or pencils, and very little paper. Often, for writing, the teacher used a stick of charcoal on a piece of birch bark. If pens were used at all, they were cut from goose quills, and the ink was homemade by the schoolmaster. The students usually sat on hard benches, while the schoolmaster stood at a high desk.

There were few books. During most of the Colonial period young schoolchildren in New England used a hornbook. This was a small, flat

wooden board with a handle. To it was attached a paper upon which was printed the lesson of the day. Since the printed lesson-papers were hard to get, the pupils covered them with a clear sheet of horn to prevent them from tearing — hence the name "hornbook." Some hornbooks were very fancy and included ivory pointers. Most of them were plain and had a string through the handle so that they could be worn around the neck.

Nearly every schoolmaster had a copy of the Bible and the Book of Psalms. After the pupils had mastered their ABC's they went on to learn reading from these books. In 1690 the *New England Primer* was published. It became the popular beginners' textbook in New England and was used for about one hundred years after it first appeared. The *Primer* taught the alphabet, spelling, and religion. It contained pictures and short verses that gave the child stern moral lessons, such as,

The idle Fool
Is whipt at School.

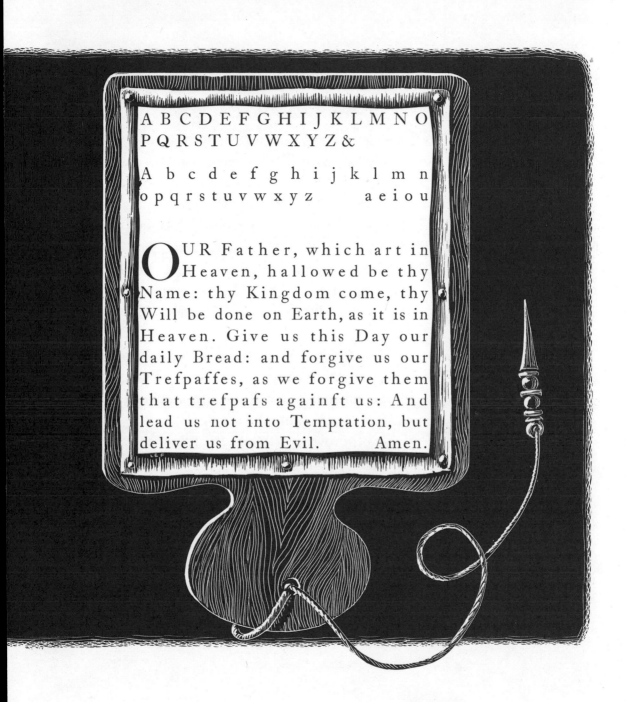

ABCDEFGHIJKLMNO
PQRSTUVWXYZ&

A b c d e f g h i j k l m n
o p q r s t u v w x y z   a e i o u

OUR Father, which art in
Heaven, hallowed be thy
Name: thy Kingdom come, thy
Will be done on Earth, as it is in
Heaven. Give us this Day our
daily Bread: and forgive us our
Trefpaffes, as we forgive them
that trefpafs againft us: And
lead us not into Temptation, but
deliver us from Evil.   Amen.

Some schools also taught writing and a little simple arithmetic. Usually one schoolmaster taught all the children of the town, even though their ages varied. Mostly the pupils memorized their lessons and did not recite as a class. Instead, they approached the schoolmaster one by one and spoke their recitations to him as he listened, standing at his high desk and keeping one eye severely on the rest of the children.

As the years went by in Colonial America, things began to happen that were to change most of the colonists' Old World ideas about government, religion, and education.

To begin with, many of the colonists who had been born in the Old World and who had brought their European customs to America had died. Their descendants, for the most part, had been born in America and were not interested in the ways of Europe or of England — places that many of them had never seen.

Besides, America was a different land from Europe. It was bigger than any single European country, and most of it was unexplored and un-

known. It still had wild areas where men, women, and children had to work hard merely to stay alive.

Then, too, the colonies were growing. At first, in many parts of America, the people had lived in little settlements clustered around the church, which was the all-important center of the community. As the years went by, however, some people moved out from the towns to the open spaces. The church was farther away from them. It no longer overshadowed them.

There was a new feeling in the air, too. In Europe the thinkers and the scientists were objecting to the limits that the Church put on their freedom of thought, and were resenting more and more the authority of the ruling classes. In no time at all the same ideas spread to America. People began to demand more freedom of every kind, and the established church began to lose its hold on them.

Besides all this, many of the colonists were beginning to know prosperity. They had grown rich by trading in slaves, salt fish, lumber, rum, molasses, and tobacco. Their new wealth brought

with it a growing feeling of independence. Their
wealth brought more leisure, too. Now there were
many printing presses in the colonies, and printed newspapers, almanacs, and sermons were ap-
pearing everywhere. There was a broadened
interest in reading.

More and more people were coming to America.
They expected something better there than in
the Old World, and they meant to have it. But
sometimes it seemed as if there was nothing but
rules and regulations and taxes.

The government in England regulated the
Colonial authorities. The Colonial authorities
regulated the people. And the people, unless they
owned land, were not allowed even to vote in
their own affairs. Soon a great deal of grumbling
was heard throughout the English colonies. The
ruling class of wealthy landowners, rich mer-
chants, and church and government officials complained of the way in which they were being
treated by the English. They resented the British
taxes and the British restrictions on trade. The
schoolmasters, sailors, farmers, clerks, and others
of their kind complained of the way in which

both England and the Colonial ruling class were treating them.

One of the loudest complaints was about schools influenced by the Church. Although the people were still religious, they came to believe that in schools where religion was all-important their children were not being taught all the things they needed to know. The education was much too narrow for their growing world. The people wanted the schools to be separated from the church and they wanted better schoolmasters.

Private schoolmasters began to appear. Many of them taught only one subject: writing, perhaps, or oratory, or English composition. They set up shop in their own homes, and pupils came to them for lessons.

In 1749, Benjamin Franklin issued a pamphlet in which he said that navigation, surveying, mathematics, chemistry, history, physics, languages, and civics must be taught to more people if the colonies were to become strong. The world was changing swiftly, the colonies were growing fast, and the old ways were no longer the best ways. Young schoolchildren must be better prepared if they were to study the subjects Franklin wrote about.

In 1751, Franklin became a trustee of an academy in Philadelphia. Here boys could still learn Latin and Greek, in order to be able to study for the ministry at a college later on. But they could study a variety of other subjects as well: arithmetic, algebra, geometry, business methods, English, and oratory. No religious subjects were taught at the academy. Soon similar academies were founded elsewhere, and the Latin grammar schools began to disappear.

In 1755, Franklin's academy joined the College of Philadelphia, founded thirteen years before. It was the first college in America not sponsored by any church. It has since become the University of Pennsylvania.

By 1770, America had nine colleges and numerous academies. Although all but one of these schools had been founded by a particular church group, now members of other groups could attend their classes. The old Puritan idea of a strict established church that had no room for outsiders had disappeared.

Scores of young men educated at the colleges began to appear all over the colonies as schoolmasters. Some were ministers waiting for an assignment. Some were biding their time, hoping that a better job of some sort might come along. Some really wanted to be schoolmasters.

Most of them did not behave differently from some of the less educated schoolmasters. They demanded absolute silence and no laughter in the classroom. They thrashed pupils here, cuffed them there, and flogged them in public whenever the occasion demanded. In return, they themselves were sometimes flogged. Nevertheless, they did bring a sense of learning and knowledge to the Colonial schoolhouse — something that had not been there before. They taught many more subjects than the early schoolmasters had. And more than that, they showed their young pupils that learning and knowledge were important and that there should be no limit to learning as long as a person wanted to go on and was able to.

It was not easy to teach school during Colonial times. It was not easy to learn, either. In fact, not until after America became an independent na-

tion were the people able to improve their education greatly.

There were some men during the Colonial period who had no more ability to teach young children than a chimpanzee would have. Yet there were other men whose education and love of knowledge and of young people made them especially fitted to teach schoolchildren.

Such a man was Nathan Hale of Connecticut, a scholar and a graduate of Yale College. He became a schoolmaster for no other reason than to give children a taste of knowledge, a love of life, liberty, and country, and a chance to be something in the New World — something more than ignorance would allow. Nathan Hale believed in these aims. In 1776, as a captain in Knowlton's Rangers of the Continental Army, he gave his life on a spying mission during which he disguised himself as a schoolmaster and used his college diploma as his credentials to pass through the enemy lines, seeking information. Schoolmasters like him, with his ideals of liberty and learning and his willingness to make a sacrifice, helped prepare the young people of America for independence and helped to shape their country into a united nation. ᏻ᎒

Index

The text of this book has been composed on the linotype in Caslon 137. This face is derived from the great oldstyle cut by William Caslon of London in the early eighteenth century. Caslon types were used widely by American printers during the colonial period and even today it is considered to be "the finest vehicle for the conveyance of English speech that the art of the punch-cutter has yet devised."

❁

Composed by Lettick Typografic, Bridgeport

Bound by H. Wolff Book Manufacturing Company, Inc., New York